Ch

That Saturday I woke with the sun powering through my thin curtains, shining through my closed eyelids, making my eyeballs warm and squinty. Isn't it amazing that heat from the sun comes almost a hundred million miles through space, and I can feel it?

'Summer,' I announced to myself. 'And the weekend!' I added. And I laughed out loud, happy. The school tests that Miss Evans had been stressing over all year were finished. They'd gone off to be marked. We had no homework because Miss Evans said we all deserved a break, and so did she. There were only a couple of months before I finished at that school forever, with the summer holiday after that. AND it was about to be my birthday.

I kicked off my duvet and stretched. I could've had a long lie-in, but somehow, because I could, I didn't want one. I was too excited with the freedom to just lie there. So I got up.

Dad had already driven off early in his lovely big old car, 'Betsy', to chauffeur a bride and her father to a wedding venue. When I stood on tiptoe and peered out of the window over the sink, I could look down and see Mum outside. She was at the back of our flats, in what the landlord calls a 'garden', but which Mum says 'shows that man has no idea what a real garden is'.

* * *

Throw-clang-plop, throw-clang-plop, throw-clang—
'Oh, Elodie, that's such an annoying noise!' said Mum.

I was throwing a tennis ball at the metal garage door, letting it drop, then catching it back on the bounce to throw again. Having a rhythm like that helps me to think. I was thinking about my grandma. She was coming to stay soon. I saw her every week over the Internet, sitting on her chair with her shelf of trophies behind her. But I'd not seen her properly to touch as well as see since I was four years old and in Reception class. Mum hadn't seen her own mum properly for all that time either.

Throw-clang-plop.

Mum was a nurse, then she decided she wanted to be a doctor. Now she's a student, and she doesn't get paid as much for the work she does at the hospital. Because of that, Dad works at his friend's design studio as well as driving Betsy. Dad worries about Mum working too hard.

Throw-clang-plop.

So Dad, who's so thoughtful, had secretly arranged for Grandma to come and visit. That was supposed to be a lovely surprise for Mum. But my dad's not very good at lying, and Mum spotted that a big sum of money had gone from their bank account. She got straight on to her phone, telling the bank person that yes, definitely, the money had been stolen, and she was going to call the police next. So Dad had to confess what he'd done.

'No, no, Maureen, we've not been defrauded!' He was flapping his hands and making faces. 'It was *me* who took the money!'

'You!'

'Yes, but for *you*.'

'Me?'

'To pay for a plane ticket for your mother.'

'Mumma?'

'She's coming here.'

'Here?'

Honestly, you'd think Mum had a rule that she could only ever say one word at a time! She's normally full of words that fly out of her mouth fast, but she was so shocked she suddenly couldn't produce more than one at a time. She soon got on to two words, though.

'Oh, Dermot!' she said, and she sat down hard. I think both Dad and I were watching her face, wondering which way it would go. She burst into tears, and that's something I'd *never* seen before. But there was soon a smile as well as the tears, and it was a big smile, so they must have been happy tears. 'Oh, Dermot, you are a lovely man!' she said at last. So Dad grinned and relaxed, and went off to polish Betsy.

Throw-clang-plop.

But Mum had been as uptight as a soap bubble that's a nanosecond away from bursting ever since then. Shouldn't she have been relaxed and happy about seeing her 'mumma' again after so long?

Throw-clang-plop, throw-clang-plop, throw—

'Elodie, mind those pots!'

Mum had planted terracotta pots of yellow and purple pansies either side of Betsy's garage door. Now she was angrily crashing a little fork into the stony ground beside the garage, levering up dandelions with long roots.

'The flowers are pretty,' I told her, trying to cheer her up.

Mum stopped digging for a moment, wiped the hair from her eyes with the back of her hand and said, 'Oh, Elodie, you should see Grandma's garden full of flowers in Trinidad. And smell it. Those red hibiscus flowers have such sweet nectar they have butterflies hovering all round! I'm ashamed of this place.' She almost closed her eyes, then opened them, looked at her own pansy pots and shook her head as she went back to digging. 'Ashamed and embarrassed, when I so want to make my mother proud!'

Throw-clang-plop.

I knew just how she felt. I so wanted to make *my* mum proud too, but I always seemed to get things wrong. I felt a sort of panic inside now, wanting to help Mum get everything right for Grandma's visit. And to help Dad. He had spent just about all our money on Grandma's plane ticket to make Mum happy, and I could see that his plan wasn't properly working. Poor Dad! Poor Mum! I tried to think of the things that definitely would make Mum happy. Presents?

Throw-clang-plop.

When I was five, I made Mum a pasta necklace at school, and she really loved it. She even wore it once. But it rained so the paint ran off the pasta beads, all down her chest like runny mascara down cheeks, but multicoloured. And then the pasta went soggy. It got thrown away. See? I couldn't even make a pasta necklace that worked!

Throw-clang-plop.

I sighed. Actually, what Mum likes more than just about anything is plants and gardening. She loves gardening with a passion. She sometimes says things like, 'If only we could have a proper garden, I'd feel we had a proper home again.' We moved from a house to a flat, you see, when Mum went back to being a student and not earning as much. I had to give up Fred the guinea pig when we moved, as well as Mum losing her garden.

Throw-clang-plop.

Nobody was really allowed to make any changes to the scrubby bit of grass and weeds and stones behind the flats. Mum says that gardens should be all about change. 'Every day new things bloom and old ones die. Every season has its different colours. And always there are plans and planting to make it better and better.' She has what Dad calls her 'faraway look' on her face whenever she talks like that about gardening.

Throw-clang-plop.

She didn't have that look now. Her mouth was tightly pushed together, and she was digging a skinny row of earth along the edge of the garage wall, trying to make 'a bit of colour'. Mum was right that Grandma loves colour. She's always wearing dresses bright with orange and pink and lime green and deep blue flowers. It's almost as if waves of colour come streaming off her. I remember that feeling from our last hug, when I was still so small my head was pressed into her lovely pillowy tummy.

Mum said those flowerpots should be OK with the landlord, because they were by Betsy's garage door and we paid rent for the garage – and because the pots were on top of the garden rather than doing anything *in* the actual garden soil. But I reckoned she was pushing her luck by digging a skinny flower bed alongside the garage wall.

'I'm just defining its boundary with colour,' is how she put it.

Throw-clang-plop, throw-clang-plop—

'Please do stop that, Elodie. We'll have the neighbours out to complain at the noise, and then they'll see what I'm doing, and then Mr Singh will get to hear about me gardening, and then – ' Mum sighed. So I caught the ball and held it.

'Shall I do some digging?' I said.

'No! Thank you, Elodie,' said Mum, trying to give me a smile. She didn't trust me to not make a mess of it. 'Just play a quieter game with that ball, would you?'

So I changed to playing keepy-uppy, knocking the ball up with my knees: right, left, right, left … CRASH!

'Oh, Elodie!' wailed Mum.

I'd smashed one of the pansy pots! It lay in pieces, the pansies and soil splatted and spilled like some sort of garden-pot car crash.

Mum made a whimpering sound. 'I *just* wanted to show my mother that I know how to make a nice home. She always did that for us. So neat, so clean, so bright, while this … ' She waved a hand at the mess and then out to include the whole scruffy area and the flats and even me.

'I'm SO sorry, Mum!' I said, and I knelt down to pick up the pieces of pot but – 'Ouch!' – I cut a finger on a sharp edge, adding blood to the soil and flowers and broken pot. Mum sort of straightened up, going into brisk ex-nurse, almost-doctor mode. She looked at the finger and made a face. 'Go and rinse that under a tap, then put on a plaster. I'll clear this mess up.'

So I went indoors, squeezing my finger and wishing I could do something right to help my mum for once, instead of spoiling things for her. That sunshine seemed to have disappeared.

Chapter Two

I climbed up the three smelly staircases to our flat, squeezing my bleeding, throbbing finger. I kept the key to our flat on a string around my neck, so I let myself in, then went to the sink. The breakfast bowls and plates were stacked either side of the sink, drying, and I made sure not to send them tumbling. Honestly – it wasn't just *me* that was the problem, even though, usually, it was mostly me. Our flat was so small it was hard for anybody to move without knocking into something.

I turned on the tap and let the cold water catch the blood from my finger, swirling it into a red feather sort of shape, before it was slurped away down the plughole and on, down inside the wall of all the flats, then along under the road – but then what? Is my blood now out at sea – invisible molecules of it travelling around the world? Maybe my finger blood will go to Trinidad before the rest of me ever does?

I climbed on to a chair to reach the first-aid box on top of the food cupboard and found a plaster. I could see through the dirty window (nobody cleans the outsides of our windows) to where Mum was on her hands and knees. She looked tiny beside the even tinier dots of colour in her pots, amongst the mostly greys and browns of the worn grass and the garages and paving stones and sheds beyond. I was just wishing that I could magic what I was seeing into a proper garden with vegetables and trees and big flower plants, when – CRASH! I fell off the chair, bumping my chin on the sink as I fell, and knocked off one of the breakfast bowls that SMASHED on the floor beside me.

'Ow! You are so clumsy!' I told myself.

Why couldn't I do *anything* right? Mum had told me so many times not to climb up on things exactly because I might fall. And now I'd got a bruised chin as well as blood drops down me.

I'm often a mess. Mum sighs and says, 'I so *want* to be proud of you, Elodie,' when she makes me change my socks so that they at least match. She tells me: 'When I was a girl, my mother always dressed me and my sisters in spotless white socks, with ribbons in our hair, wearing the bright cotton dresses she made us.' Then she looks at me in my shorts and T-shirt and frizzy ginger hair that hasn't been brushed and shakes her head. I'm not the sort of daughter proud parents dream of in other ways, either. I hardly ever come top in any school test. In one writing test not long ago, I didn't notice the "n't" – meaning "not" – in the title question, "Why Shouldn't We Bully One Another?", so I wrote all about why we *should* bully one another. Everybody in the class, even Toby who's my best friend, laughed when they heard what I'd done. I tried to pretend I thought it was funny too, but I was mortified. I really thought I'd done a good answer for once. In fact, Miss Evans said I had thought of some good ideas. But because they weren't answers to the actual question, she couldn't give any marks for them. And the spelling was rubbish too, of course. It always is, in spite of me getting extra one-to-one help with it. I did once get a certificate, though – for the 'Best Recycling Idea'. Mum helped me make a garden on a tray full of old teacups planted with parsley and nasturtiums. It was pretty, and you could eat the flowers as well as the parsley!

Anyway, at least I did manage to clear up the broken bowl without cutting myself again. As I dustpan-and-brushed the bits up, I tried to think of a way to make Mum so proud of me that her own mother, my grandma, would be proud of her, and then all three generations of us would be happy. But what, what, what could I, Elodie Taylor, *achieve*? That was the question. If I *really* tried with my homework, could I ever get the best mark in a spelling test? That's a dull sort of achievement though, I thought. I wanted to do something sparkly and exciting, to make everyone feel really proud of me, in a surprised sort of way.

Mum caught me – dustpan of bowl bits in my hand, first-aid kit all over the floor, red sore patch blooming on my bruised chin. My thoughts slammed back to where I actually was.

'Sorry, Mum,' I said. 'Big proper sorry, sorry, sorry,' which was pathetic, but I didn't know what else to say.

Mum put an arm round me. 'No, *I'm* sorry,' she said. 'Your dad and I are a bit fraught at the moment, and that's not your fault. How's your finger?' I held it up, showing her the plaster.

'Good job,' said Mum. 'I'll finish clearing up here, and could you please go down to the shop? We need eggs for lunch. Here – take a bit extra from my purse and get yourself a treat of a magazine or something.'

'To make my finger better?' I grinned, and she smiled back. We were all right again.

When I was little, a Mum kiss on a 'hurty' thing worked better than anything else at making that hurt go. Then, from when I was about six to nine, being bought a treat did the same sort of magic. But I'm almost eleven now, and it seems that just the *idea* of a treat is enough to cheer me up. Will that work once I'm properly grown-up?

So I went down our road towards the row of shops. There's a nail bar and a hairdresser's, and then there's 'the' shop that has newspapers and some food and shoelaces and things, and we go to it most days for something or other.

I looked at the comics, trying to choose one, but they were babyish. Mum had said 'magazine', so I looked at those, but they were all talking about how to look gorgeous in a pouty lipsticky way, so not worth the effort of reading. I could have got something to eat as a treat, I suppose. There were plastic-wrapped chocolate muffins, but I knew they wouldn't be anywhere near as nice as the ones Mum makes.

Then an old lady said to me: 'You're a nice tall girl. Would you be very kind and reach me down that packet of brown sugar?' So I went on to tiptoes and got it down for her.

'Thank you so much,' said the lady, all big smiles. If only being good and making *Mum* happy was as easy as that!

Then I thought, *Could I use the treat money to buy Mum a present?* But that would be weird, wouldn't it? Taking from her to give to her? The idea felt like cheating or stealing, but it wasn't truly either of those things ... was it? If I took the two or three pounds she wanted me to spend on a magazine and used it on her, that actually would make me happier than buying a magazine, so that works right, doesn't it? But it somehow didn't feel right, so I just bought the eggs and headed back home with the change to go back in Mum's purse. I was walking back home when I saw a friend of mine.

'Reginald,' I said, stopping to admire him. 'You do know that you are the handsomest ever, don't you?' I could see from his face that he *did* know that. I stroked his silky hair and tickled under his chin.

Reginald is a cat, by the way, just in case you hadn't realized. And 'Reginald' is just the name I chose to call him. I didn't know what his real one was. But you can't talk to somebody properly without using a name, so I'm always making up names for cats or birds or dogs I meet. This cat was fat and old and lovely: black, with white under his chin and on three of his paws and the end of his tail. He'd found a hot spot on the tall wall that divides the pavement from an overgrown garden, and he sort of slopped saggily over the bricks as if he was an aubretia plant. Reginald didn't seem to mind the traffic or the people on our side of the wall. He just lay there, his eyes almost closed and a smug look on his face, not actually caring if he was admired or ignored.

Aren't cats wonderful, the way they don't care what anybody else thinks of them? I'd like to be a cat. I'd really like to have one, too. It's so soothing just stroking and stroking a cat's silky soft fur, and so flattering if they choose to look you in the eye and smile and maybe even purr.

That's it! I thought. *What Mum needs is a cat to make her relax.*

Chapter Three

Reginald's purring mixed with purring of another kind, and I realized that Dad had drawn up Betsy to the kerb beside me, his driver window wound down.

'Want a lift?' he said. We'd only got a short way to go, but it's always been a treat for me to ride in that lovely, grand old car. It's true that I looked up and down the pavement, just to check that nobody from school was watching – because it *is* a bit of an embarrassing car – but, 'Yes, please,' I said.

Betsy is a soft, light-green colour and enormous – especially in the front part where the big old engine is. There's a big silver radiator on the very front, with a metal winged shape sitting on the nose of the car. Even though Betsy is such a big car, it only has one door each side. I usually have to tip the front seat over so that I can climb into the back, but with no Mum in the car today I went in the front passenger seat. There were white ribbons forming a 'V' from the winged shape at the front of the bonnet, because Betsy had been working at a wedding that morning.

The leather seats are big and so shiny that you slide over them. You have to wind a handle to make the window go down. Toby couldn't believe it the first time he had a ride in Betsy.

'This car must be ancient,' he said. 'Greek or Roman or something. Perhaps Stone Age?'

It's actually only about sixty-five years old, but that's still much older than even my dad.

'I've got an idea,' I told Dad, as I sat and shut the door. 'Mum needs a cat.'

'Ah,' said Dad. 'I saw you talking to that one on the wall.'

'Cats are so calming and lovely,' I said.

'I don't think that's a good idea,' said Dad.

'Oh. Don't you like cats, then?'

'I love them,' said Dad, pulling on the shiny wooden steering wheel to turn us right into the lane beside our flats. 'We always had cats back at the farm where I grew up. The best one of them all was called Puisìn. That's Irish for "puss".' He pronounced it so that it sounded like 'pwisheen'.

'Then why can't we—'

'Mum would say no, and she'd be right,' said Dad. 'Remember that we've got your grandma coming to visit soon.'

'Doesn't Grandma like cats, then?'

'I've no idea about that,' said Dad. 'But I do know that you're going to have to move out of your room when Grandma's here. Do you think you'd be OK on the sofa?' Dad frowned. 'Although that would be awkward with bedtimes. Maybe you should share the big bed with Mum, and I'll go on the sofa?'

'I wish—' I began, wishing that we had an extra bedroom for Grandma.

'I do too,' said Dad quickly, flicking on the indicator that made a little arm with a light on it shoot out of the side of the car and flash to show we were turning towards the garages. 'And one day we will move to a bigger place again.' Dad works at the studio during the week, but I know his dream is to just work with Betsy and maybe other old cars. Then he shocked me by saying quietly, 'I suppose I should just sell Betsy really.'

'You can't do that! You love Betsy! And so do I,' I said, stroking the seat leather in case Betsy felt upset at what Dad had said.

Betsy is beautiful. She belonged to Dad's dad and his grandad before that. His – my great grandad's – wife was called Betsy, and he named the car after her, the way people sometimes name their boats after loved ones. We've got a photo of Dad when he was little, wearing red shorts, long before he was a dad, standing beside Betsy.

He has his hand on her big bonnet, with his dad and his grandad in the car seats behind: all three of them looking as proud and happy about that car as, well, as I wish Mum and Dad felt about me.

'She's expensive to run, and the truth is that not many people want to be driven about in a car like this nowadays,' said Dad.

'But ... weddings!' I said.

'Yes, weddings are my main jobs with Betsy these days, but there aren't enough of them to do much more than cover the cost of running her.'

'What about pop stars?' I said. Dad had a few stories about famous pop stars Grandad used to drive around. But Dad shook his head.

'Not any more, it seems. They all want air conditioning and tinted windows these days. Can you imagine if Betsy had tinted windows? It wouldn't be right, even if I could afford it. The truth is, Elodie, that we're going to be tight for money until your mum qualifies as a doctor. I should sell Betsy to a collector, then buy a cheap little car for us.'

'But you'd miss Betsy so much!' I said.

'I would,' said Dad. 'She's my pride and joy. It would feel like selling a member of the family.' He gave a little laugh. 'She's a beauty and a friend. But, after all, she – or rather "it" – is only a car.'

'You can fetch Grandma from the airport in Betsy, and that'll make Mum proud,' I said.

'Hop out and open the garage door, would you, love?' said Dad. And that was the end of that conversation.

Could a child, even one who was almost at secondary school, ever earn enough money to make a difference to our family finances? I know the shop doesn't allow you to do a paper round until you're fourteen. That's a few years away for me. There are lottery cards for sale in the shop, but the chances of winning anything big are 'about the same as the chance of picking a golden flea off your dog', according to Dad. Besides, I don't think you're even allowed to buy lottery tickets until you're sixteen. It's really not fair! What chance do I have of really helping my family? The *only* thing I could do would be to become Mum and Dad's 'pride and joy', like Betsy was, to at least make them feel a bit better.

Chapter Four

It was Book Week at school, and that always ended with an assembly where people won things. I knew there'd be a certificate for the person who wrote the best story. I couldn't do that with my bad spelling. There'd be another certificate for the person who read the most books in the week. But I'd always been really slow at reading compared to most of the others in the class. If I started reading before the week even began, perhaps I could have got through lots of books and reviewed them all. If I just put in a lot more time than anybody else, I should have been able to win that one, shouldn't I? You might think that I could just pretend to read books and not really do it. But Miss Evans was clever about that. She'd read just about everything in the world, and she always asked you tricksy questions. But even if I couldn't cheat, I could be cunning. So I went to the bookcase in the main room and chose a short book, but an adult one, because I knew that would impress Miss Evans. I chose *The Snow Goose* by Paul Gallico. Then I spent all of Sunday struggling to read it. I lay on my bed, then sat on the floor, then sat in Dad's armchair – draped like a wave over its two arms – then walked about with the book open. Slowly, the page numbers went up. I read past my usual bedtime, but by the time I fell asleep with the book, splat, over my face, there were still seventeen pages left to read.

I woke and realized that I'd failed to read even that one short book over an empty day, so what chance did I have of reading a record number of books in the days filled with school in the rest of that week? I thought again about trying to lie by saying that I had finished lots of books, and if Miss Evans tested me on their endings, I could say I'd read so many in such a short time I just couldn't remember everything about them. But I'm as rubbish at lying as I am at spelling or doing things without breaking myself or objects. When it was my third birthday, Mum made me a cake with coloured sweets on top in a circle like beads on a necklace. When she left me alone in the kitchen with the cake for a moment, I couldn't resist stealing the red sweet. Mum came in, saw the cake and asked me, 'Elodie, did you take that sweet?'

'No,' I said.

'Then where can it have gone?' said Mum.

And I said, 'Into my tummy, maybe?'

See? Hopeless. I knew Miss Evans would see straight through me. What, then? I should give up trying to read lots of books, that's what. I couldn't win that certificate, so why bother even trying?

Miss Evans had said that we were going to have half hours of reading time each morning and afternoon of Book Week, and that we could use that time to read anything we liked. Well, I'd had enough of *The Snow Goose*, now that it couldn't win me anything, so I decided to take a book about the human body and diseases that had lots of pictures. I *can* read pictures fine. It's one of Mum's medical books. It's got photographs showing juicy sores and wonky broken limbs and scabby patches. It's horrible, but also fascinating.

So I was shoving *The Illustrated Medical Dictionary* into my school bag when I found a crumpled bit of paper. I opened it out:

Dear Parents and Guardians,
We are going to have a 'dress as a book character' day as part of our school Book Week.

Oh, no! I'd forgotten all about the dressing-up thing! I didn't want to be the only person turning up in a grey skirt and a green jumper with the school emblem tree picture done years ago by somebody from Nursery. It made me feel instant panic fizzing in my fingers and knotting me inside when I thought of how everyone would laugh if I was the only one not in costume. I just knew that the other girls in my class would be looking amazing. I'd heard Grace and Usma planning to come as characters from

Alice in Wonderland. They were going to be the Rabbit and Alice, one with proper face-paint whiskers and fluffy ears, and the other with a big bow in their hair. Everyone would be looking at them.

'Mum!' I said. 'I've got to dress up as a book character. Now!' I fluttered the note at her.

'Oh, Elodie, why didn't you give that to me before?' She said it in that exasperated mum way. She'd got her phone tucked under her chin – her head on one side to clamp it in place while her hands were flying to the fridge and the cutlery drawer and spreading and slicing and making sandwiches for my lunch. She'd rung the council and they'd put her on hold. 'I haven't got time to start making costumes now. We've got to be out of here in the next five minutes if I'm going to make it to my lecture on time.' Dad had already left really early as he had an important presentation to prepare.

'Do you want tomato with your cheese?' said Mum. 'A banana or apple? Oh, hello? Yes, sorry, I was talking to my daughter.' And Mum's brain had switched off me again and on to whoever was on the phone. I knew I'd just have to sort a costume for myself.

What could I do? Lots of the girls would be in Hermione costumes of black gowns with crests on them, as if the Hogwarts school uniform had become ours for the day. The boys too, of course, would be dressed as

Harry with a lightning zigzag on their foreheads. I knew that Toby would do something simple and clever. I hadn't asked him, but I just know how he thinks. And Lola would be looking brilliant in some fantastic original costume that her artist dad had made for her. Last year she came as The Great Glass Elevator, complete with a lift that wound up and down with a handle.

What could I be? In almost no time at all? I rummaged at the bottom of my wardrobe where I kept odd things I'd grown out of but was still too fond of to throw away when we moved to the flat. There was a princess dress from when I was about six years old. I pulled it out. It was babyish and had a tear on its green skirt. Could I be Tinkerbell from *Peter Pan*, with her very short green fairy dress? I took off my school uniform, stepped into the little green dress and tried to pull it up my body. *Riiip!* It was way too short, way too tight and, well, just wrong in every way.

Help! What book character could I turn a tall girl with ginger Afro hair and freckles into? Mum comes from Trinidad, so that's why I have Afro hair, but the ginger is from Dad, who's from Ireland. I get my freckles from him too. Anne of Green Gables is ginger-haired and with freckles, but not Afro hair. Maybe Princess Merida? But I hadn't got a bow and arrow. And is she even from a book as well as a film? I peeled off the ruined green dress and threw it into the bin. Then I did have an idea. I could go as a doctor, and that would fit with the medical book I was taking into school. Brilliant! I could slip on a pair of Mum's blue scrubs. 'Scrubs' is what they call the baggy trousers and tops they wear on some wards. Really simple and comfortable (if I rolled the sleeves and legs up). Perfect. But ...

'Sorry, Elodie,' said Mum. 'Those scrubs don't come home with me. They're washed at the hospital.'

'Mum! Then what *can* I wear?' The clock was ticking on, as clocks and time always do, whether you want them to or not.

'I can't conjure something out of thin air, can I?' said Mum. 'You should have told me about this before.' I already knew that. Mum tutted, brushing off some Crispie Pops that had somehow stuck to my chin. 'Look at you – you're such a mess!' she said. And suddenly another idea arrived in my brain. *Ping!* And because of the way this idea had arrived, I knew I could make it work.

'I'll be Mrs Twit!'

'Who?' said Mum.

'Mrs Twit from *The Twits*! She's a really disgusting mess. I can do that.'

'Well, hurry up, will you,' said Mum, taking her coat off its hook. 'We're going to be late.'

So I did the quickest change ever. I pulled on my dad's huge old Mending the Car and Other Dirty Jobs Jumper.

It's grey, blotched with smelly old black oil and it's got holes in it. Mum's always wanting Dad to throw it out. She's bought him new jumpers, but Dad always says he'll wear the old one 'just one more time', and it never is the last time, so he's still got it. Anyway, it was perfect for Mrs Twit. It reached down to my knees – baggy and saggy and just a bit smelly. I quickly stuck Crispie Pops on to my face with honey to be warts. I stuck more into my hair. Then I blopped a glug of ketchup down my front.

'Oh, Elodie, do you have to?' said Mum.

'Yup,' I said. 'After this, Dad really *will* get rid of this jumper, so I'm doing you a favour.' I took the walking stick from next to the front door, which my dad's mum had left last time she visited, as Mum handed me my bag. I screwed my face on one side so that one eye was almost closed and the other open, and I was doing a sort of snarling grin.

'Oh, honestly, Elodie!' said Mum, laughing. 'Come on. We are seriously late now.'

Chapter Five

I didn't even mind being late. I quite wanted to 'make an entrance', as Miss Evans would call it. I knew that everyone would turn from their tables and look, and they'd all laugh at my Mrs Twit outfit, and I'd laugh too. There's such a difference, isn't there, between being laughed at when you're *wanting* to make people laugh and being laughed at when you're trying to look serious and nice? This time I'd be getting the laughs for the right reason.

I hobbled with my stick and my bag and my screwed-up sideways face down the road. It was fun seeing people in cars pointing at me and laughing!

We *were* late. The others had all gone inside already, just as I'd sort of hoped that they would.

'Go on,' said Mum, giving me a push. 'Apologize to Miss Evans. Have a lovely day, and remember, you're going home with Toby.'

'Bye, Mum!'

In I went. The office lady buzzed me through. She was on the phone, and her jaw dropped open like a fish when she saw me. That made *me* laugh. Then I pushed through into my classroom, first door on the right ...

... and there sat everyone at the tables – every single one of them in the grey and green school uniform.

I froze. They froze.

Then they started to laugh. They really, really laughed, looking at me and then each other, hands to mouths in wonder at the look of me. And, no, they weren't laughing *with* me because I was deliberately looking funny. They were laughing *at* me because there I stood – ketchup and Crispie Pops down my front, in my hair and stuck on to my face – ON THE WRONG DAY!

Miss Evans tried to make it all right. She found some old PE kit from Lost Property for me to change into, so I sat in too-big blue shorts that smelled a bit funny and a too-small white T-shirt. I'm not sure that it was any better than Dad's stinky old jumper. I pulled the Crispie-Pops warts off my face, but they left sticky spots. And I couldn't get rid of all the ones in my hair. I'd been a bit over-enthusiastic when I stuck them in, I suppose. I found more and more of them still there all through the day. People kept pointing them out to me, or throwing pencil sharpenings and chips into my hair to make me 'look even more like Mrs Twit'. I promise you, that Monday was *the* slowest school day *ever* in the history of time! Sometimes clocks do go slowly.

I went home with Toby after school. Toby's been my friend since we were babies, a bit like a brother because we know each other so well. Our mums have been friends since antenatal classes, so you could say we've been friends since we were foetuses. Anyway, Toby tried to cheer me up.

'But it *was* funny, Elodie!' he kept telling me.

'Yeah, well, I'm glad I made you all happy,' I said, but I didn't mean it. I felt as if I didn't want to go back to school ever. At least, not that school and that class. It wasn't long until it would be the end of primary school forever. 'Perhaps I'll pretend to be ill until it's September and time to start at secondary school?' Then I went quiet as we walked to Toby's house, the rhythm of our steps helping me to think.

'Elodie?' said Toby.

'I'm thinking,' I said.

'About what?'

I sighed. 'Just about how I'm rubbish at everything. I'm a joke at this school, and I'm going to get everything wrong all the time and be a joke at the next school too, aren't I?' Toby didn't say anything. 'Dad's talking about selling Betsy,' I told him. 'And Mum's uptight because *her* mum's coming to stay, and our flat's too small for the three of us, let alone having an extra person who will find the stairs difficult. And Mum has to work too hard. And Dad doesn't earn enough.' Toby was still silent. 'I just think that if they could be proud of me for something, they wouldn't mind all those other things so much. Anyway, that's the only thing I can think of to help, and I can't even do it because I'm useless at everything, aren't I?' And, again, Toby didn't deny it. That's what I love about Toby. He doesn't tell lies to try and make you feel better. Somehow, the fact that he's being honest with you makes you feel a teeny bit better anyway.

Then we got to Toby's house and Toby's dad opened the door, putting a finger to his lips to tell us to shush. He beckoned us, tiptoeing into their living room, where he pointed to a cardboard box full of an old jumper, Toby's cat Mabel and ...

'Oh!'

'Kittens!' said Toby.

'Two of them,' said Toby's dad. 'Keep quiet, and you can watch. I think there's more to come.'

Toby's little sister Cherry was there, watching too. Their dad brought us drinks and biscuits and we sat and watched, mostly in silence, as Mabel licked the two damp tiny kittens that were already born, and her body heaved every now and again in a way Toby's dad said meant she was getting ready to have another one. Mabel is a patchwork of ginger and black-and-white, and one of her kittens was the same colour and the other was all white. They had their eyes closed and were damp and sticky-looking.

'I'm calling them Bob and Bobina,' said Cherry.

'Shush!' said Toby.

'Bob can be yours, Toby; Bobina is mine, and she's that one.' Cherry poked the tiny white kitten.

'Stop that!' said Toby. 'We don't even know whether they're boys or girls. And it isn't just you who'll name them, anyway!' And suddenly Cherry was running out of the room, calling to complain to her dad about Toby, and Toby followed her.

So it was only me there when a third kitten was born. It lay in the bottom of the cardboard box, with its eyes tightly closed. Mabel reached around to lick the new kitten, nudging it with her nose.

'Mabel, you clever girl!' I whispered.

I didn't want to touch the kitten, with its funny little face, pink nose and flattened little triangle ears.

'Breathe, little one!' I whispered. I didn't shout out for Toby. I almost held my breath. I just had such a feeling of this being *my* kitten because the other two belonged to Toby and Cherry, so I was selfish, wanting to be the only person in the world who knew about that kitten – just for a few more moments. Mabel licked its damp gingery head, and suddenly its limp little body moved and the kitten opened its mouth to silently take a first breath. I've never ever seen anything so wonderful in my whole life.

In one part of my brain, I was already wondering how to persuade Mum and Dad to let me have that kitten, knowing the answer would almost certainly be 'no'. But another part of my brain was saying: *Just shut up with those thoughts and make the most of this happening for real, to you, Elodie Taylor!*

Can you imagine being a kitten who's living in a squished-up nothing sort of time, growing, then being squeezed out into brightness and sounds and air and space and a mum's tongue lick, lick, licking you? I suppose it's the same as when I was born. Except for the licking bit. I wish I could remember that first taste of air. Opening my eyes and *seeing* for the first time! The best present ever and I don't even remember it! Mum and Dad certainly remember me being born, so why can't I, when it's the same number of years ago for me as for them, and I'm the one with the young brain that's supposed to work best? Mum always says that me being born was *her* best present ever, and now I can see why. Giving birth is a bit like unwrapping a present, but a living present! Oh, I wanted, wanted, wanted that kitten!

It can only have been a minute or two before the others were back in the room, then they called their dad, and of course the little ginger kitten belonged to all of them, and to Mabel, and I knew I was just a lucky bystander.

However that moment of birth and first breath *were* just mine, even if I never got more of the kitten than that.

'This new one's going to be called Bobinella,' said Cherry.

'Don't poke it!' said Toby.

'I think it's time we all left this little family in peace,' said Toby's dad.

So Toby and I went up to his bedroom. I know his room well, but this time I really noticed the shelf on his bookcase that was full of trophy cups and medals and a team photo. That shelf looked like the ones that are always behind Grandma when we talk online. She'll sometimes point to a new medal or certificate and tell me which of her Trinidadian or American grandchildren had won that one and what for.

'There's you,' I said to Toby, pointing to the boy with the curls on his head in the football team picture. 'Wow, I didn't know you'd won so many cups!'

'Yeah, well I'm just good at all those things, aren't I?' said Toby, sounding bored.

'Well, there is one thing you're completely rubbish at,' I said.

'What?'

'Being modest!'

'I'm just being honest, aren't I?' said Toby.

And, actually, that's true. What's so good about lying and pretending not to be so good when you actually are so good? I'd seen Toby collecting the trophy cups at the sort of school assemblies when parents get invited.

'You must be your parents' pride and joy,' I said. 'I wish that I could win something and get a trophy.'

'Do it, then,' said Toby. 'You're OK at some sports.'

And, because Toby *is* an honest person, just for a moment I believed him enough to feel a flutter of possibility. Then reality thumped me in the gut with a memory of me in a football match, kicking the ball into our team's goal. I'd certainly got that wrong.

'What you mean is that I'm not as rubbish at some sports as I am at literacy and all that other stuff,' I said.

'No,' said Toby. 'Actually, you're a really fast runner.'

It's true that I'm taller than most of the other girls my age, so I can run faster than lots of them. But I don't run as effortlessly as Grace in school does. She looks like one of those antelopes you see on television sometimes: running really fast but looking as though it's in slow motion somehow, legs reaching further than anybody else's, feet grabbing the ground and pushing behind her. Dad says I look like an octopus trying to tap dance, always tripping myself up with my own legs. I've tried making my legs go wider apart from each other so that they don't trip each other up, but that just made everybody hysterical, laughing at me … again.

'You're way better than I am at running, Toby.'

'True,' said Toby. 'But there is one thing you are actually better at than I am.'

'What's that?'

'Swimming.'

That was true. You know how penguins and seals waddle awkwardly on land, then dive around the place as smoothly as fish once they're under water? I'm a bit like that. I love that feeling of being supported by the water, yet free within it to do somersaults or walking-on-the-moon kind of long, slow leaps. Or swimming at the surface of the water, with the rhythm of the arms and legs and breathing all making it easy to think. With swimming, Miss Evans isn't marking you for whether you get it right or wrong; you just do it. Yup, I actually like swimming.

'You should try out for the swimming team,' said Toby. 'Remember? We had a letter about it last week to take home.' That letter was probably still in my bag. 'The trials are straight after the school holidays,' said Toby. 'I'm going in for it. It's for the Primary School Swimming Gala at the big pool the first Saturday after half-term. Do you know if you are free then?'

'Yes, I think so. Yes, I'll do it too! Toby Wythenshaw, you just might have found a way for me to make my family proud.' Then I remembered something else. 'Can we go and have another little look at the kittens before I go home?'

Mabel had washed the third kitten clean of gunk, and all three kittens were now lined up at her tummy, ready to feed but fast asleep. 'My' kitten was beautiful – ginger all over except for the pink splodge of nose. So sweet! If only!

I walked home from Toby's in a haze of daydream, imagining Grandma holding my swimming medal or cup and saying how proud she was of me, and my mum feeling proud that I'd made Grandma proud, and Dad gazing at Mum, being happy that Mum was so proud, and me gazing at Dad and ... well, you know the sort of daydream. But just add a very sweet little ginger kitten into that picture. The kitten would need to be six weeks old before it left Mabel. I'd asked Toby's dad, and he told me that. But the swimming bit of that dream could actually work, all within the next few weeks. *If* I made it happen.

I clutched my school bag and jogged the rest of the way home, even up all forty-five stairs to our flat.

I needed to be in the best possible physical condition ready for the swimming trials. I just hoped that permission letter was still in my bag.

Chapter Six

I found the letter about the swimming trials and gala, a bit crumpled but still all there, squashed under Mum's big *Illustrated Medical Dictionary* in my bag.

'Dad, can you sign this, please?' I said, handing it to him.

'Swimming team, eh?' he said as he signed it. Mum was still at college.

'Daaaad,' I said, all drawn-out and wheedling. 'Toby's cat has had kittens, and they are soooo sweet, and—'

'No,' said Dad. 'Sorry, love. But, no. Not now.'

Oh well, half a dream is better than no dream. So I went to my room and switched on my laptop to research 'swimming training'. No surprise that most swimming training involves swimming. But I hadn't got a handy swimming pool in my flat, had I! And there was no chance of a bus ride to the council pool now, with Dad already preparing dinner. So I looked on down the list of advice that didn't involve actually swimming. There was stuff about food and exercises for building muscles. There was a picture of somebody, arms out, walking along one of those wooden beams they use in the Olympics, working on balance. It said: 'Working the pectoral muscles and biceps is vital to giving your stroke the power you need for speed.' Speed was what I was after to win races. I looked up 'pectoral' and 'bicep' muscles in the medical dictionary. I turned to a page showing horribly injured and horribly diseased chest muscles that were 'pectoral' and torn arm ones which were 'biceps', so at least I knew where those muscles were. Arms needed to be strong for swimming. So I went to the kitchen and picked up two tins of soup from the cupboard, and I lifted them in turn: left, right, up and down.

'What in the world?' said Dad, trying to reach around me for a knife to chop up an onion.

'Training,' I said. 'Are you making pasta sauce?'

'Yep.'

'Wholemeal pasta?'

Dad glanced at the packet and shook his head. 'No. Why does it matter?'

'Because I need "complex carbohydrates",' I said. 'You get them in wholegrain stuff and green veg and sweet potatoes and ... phew!' I ran out of breath and clomped the soup tins down.

'Oi!' said Dad, catching a pepper I'd set rolling over and off the table.

'My arms really hurt, and that's after only about two minutes! Can I make a smoothie? The training advice says that I've got to get all the right energy and vitamins.

And proteins to build up muscles. And I can't have "nutritionally empty foods", it says.'

'So you don't want one of my toffees?' Dad waggled his eyebrows, daring me.

'No, I don't,' I said. I *really* wanted to win the swimming thing. 'I need yogurt and bananas and berries.'

'We haven't got any berries.'

'It says frozen ones are fine.'

'Well, take a look in the freezer drawer and you might find some.' I did!

'And I need oats,' I said.

'In the cereal cupboard,' said Dad, shimmying his hips out of the way so that I could reach it.

I put everything into the blender and turned it on. *Whizzz!*

'Don't forget the ... ' began Dad.

But of course, I had forgotten. The lid.

Splat, splatter ALL over the kitchen cupboards and floor and ceiling and me and ...

'Dad!' He was licking it off his arm.

'Delicious!' he said. He's so good with my disasters. I poured the nutritionally balanced dribble of smoothie that was still left in the blender into a glass. It *was* delicious, as well as nutritious. I just hoped it was propitious (that's a word Dad sometimes uses) too for getting me into the team. 'Come on,' said Dad, throwing a damp cloth at me. 'Get this lot cleaned up before Mum gets back.'

Bending and stretching to mop up and down and under the kitchen units and table was probably better exercise than the soup-can lifting had been. One day I'm going to write a best-selling book about how you can exercise while cleaning the house. It'll make me a fortune, and Mum and Dad will be so proud. But for now, I knew my best hope of Parental Pride was that swimming team.

I tried making bath time a bit of swimming practice. I ran the bath water until it was about five centimetres from the rim of the bath. When I got in, very carefully, the water rose to just a diddy bit below where it would have gone over the edge. When I slooped down in the bath I could float on my back, just so long as I kept my legs bent a bit. The website training advice said you should practise 'propulsion' even when you were not swimming along. It said: 'You could try closing your eyes so as to feel exactly how the muscles and bones work together to create a pair of human flippers from your feet.' So I closed my eyes and kick-flipped.

'Oh, Elodie!'

Mum was not amused by the water all over the floor.

But at least I got more bending and stretching and mopping exercise before I went to bed. And Dad did say he'd try to make the time to take me to the swimming pool the next day after school. He did, too, and I did as many exercises as I could remember and raced Dad and kept up with him. We went every day that week. Then on Thursday, while he cooked tea again ready for when Mum got home, I went along to the shop to fetch more milk.

When I got to the bit of pavement with the wall where I talked to Reginald sometimes, I had an idea. I remembered that picture of balance training on a beam, because the wall was at just the same sort of head height off the ground and was long and thin and hard. Luckily, there was an old chair outside the junk shop, just in front of the end of the wall. So I put the milk money in my pocket, stepped on to the chair, then reached up to one of the tree branches from the garden on the other side, and I got up on to that brick wall.

I'd forgotten all over again about Mum's warning about climbing up on things.

The wall was thin and the bricks a bit crumbly. I straightened up, and the ground shrank smaller and further away as I went up. I wobbled. Sometimes I wish I was shorter.

'Balance!' I told myself. I already had my right arm out and wavering to try and steady me, as the left hand held on to the branch. But that branch wasn't as strong and steady as it looked. It bent as I wobbled. I took a breath, then blew it out as if I was blowing out candles on a cake. I took a step, and actually keeping my balance was easier when I was moving than when I was trying to keep still, and suddenly I was doing step, step, and I'd let go of the branch and both arms were out like slightly flappy aeroplane wings, step ...

'Oh!'

Fat Reginald had jumped up, silent and smooth, then stood on the wall in front of me, looking at me with a smug catty grin.

'Re ... Reg ... i ... No!' He was nudging his face against my front leg, purring as he smarmed his whiskery cheek against me.

'Oh!'

And I fell.

Chapter Seven

I fell, crashing through scratchy twigs, on to the Dark Side of the Wall. *Wump!* For a moment I had no breath, then a sort of whimper came out of me.

'Ow!'

Something was very wrong with my left leg. It hurt in a way I'd never felt anything hurt before. In fact, it hurt so much I sort of floated away from my own hurting body and watched myself having a conversation with myself in my head: *You're in big trouble now, Elodie Taylor. What are you going to do about it?*

I don't know. Should I move?

I tried moving. 'OW!'

Not a good idea. And I could tell that my leg was bending in a direction that a leg shouldn't bend. My eyes were getting hot and my mouth was going wobbly. *Crying won't help!* I told myself. Should I shout for help? There must be people walking along the other side of the wall, on the Light Side. But they wouldn't want to sort out some stupid girl who'd fallen off a wall! Mum and Dad and Toby, and everybody who I really wanted to come and help me, weren't anywhere nearby.

Then suddenly there was a firm little nose nudging at my face, licking me with a tiny raspy tongue, at the same time as tickling me with whiskers, then – 'Mrrow!' – meowing loudly. One friend was near me, after all.

'Reg!' I whispered, and I found that I could lift one hand to stroke him and somehow that made me feel a bit better. I wanted to tell Reginald that me falling wasn't his fault, but saying anything out loud was too hard to do. I hoped that my stroking him would let him know I still loved him.

'Mrrow!' went Reginald. Then ...

'Priss!' called a voice. Reginald's ears went up. There were sort of kissing noises from over in the trees, then an old-lady voice was calling, 'Priss, whatever have you got there? I do hope it's not another poor little mouse or shrew, you naughty girl!' And the branches of the bush beside me moved apart to show a startled face, with bright white hair like a hat over the top of it.

'Oh, my goodness!' said the lady. 'It's a girl! Are you hurt?'

'Just ... well ... oh, I'm sorry to be in your garden!' Would she be cross?

'Dear, oh dear, you've come off the wall, haven't you?' said the lady. She stamped the twiggy bushes aside and seemed to swoop down on me from above. 'Who are you, my dear?' Then she looked at me sharply. 'Oh, I know you! You're the kind girl who reached down that sugar for me from the high shelf in the shop!' She looked delighted.

'Oh. Yes,' I gasped, remembering. It was hard to talk when breathing was my main job, along with stopping myself from letting that leg pain swamp me like a wave.

'I'm so glad it's you,' said the lady, which seemed an odd thing to say when it was hurting very much to be me. 'I can see that leg's a mess, but does anything else hurt?' I was bruised and scratched, but the only big thing was ...

'My leg,' I said. 'It really hurts.' And then that wave of pain did sweep over me with a sick feeling, and that's the last I remember for a bit.

It felt as if I was waking up from a sleep, sort of fuzzy and nice, until where I was and what had happened and the pain in my leg slammed into me again.

'You're awake!' said the lady. 'Good. I've asked somebody over the wall to call for an ambulance. I don't have one of those little pocket telephones. But I'm assured by a helpful boy that an ambulance is on its way. Now, let's introduce ourselves while we wait for it to arrive.' The lady smiled. 'I am Mrs Banbury. I live in the house back there, and this is a part of my garden I never normally visit. But I heard Priss calling out.'

'Priss?'

'Yes, my sometimes naughty but very lovely cat here. Priss is short for Priscilla.'

I think I smiled. It would have hurt too much to laugh. Did Reginald/Priss care that he/she was a completely different cat to the two of us? Cats don't care. Except that he/she *had* cared enough to get Mrs Banbury to help me, I think. 'Thank you,' I whispered to both of them.

'My pleasure,' said Mrs Banbury. 'This actually is a bit of an adventure for me. Ah, do you hear that?' I could hear a swooping siren sound coming closer. 'Your ambulance, I think. I'll just alert them to where we are and direct them to the gate.'

Soon there were kind people dressed in green prodding me, asking who I was and where I lived and what hurt, and I think they gave me an injection. And then I was on a bed sort of thing and being carried over the bushes, through a gateway, and up into an ambulance. They said they'd called Dad, and he was on his way to the hospital, and they told me not to worry about anything. I was inside the ambulance and that was interesting. There was a chair sideways on to me that an ambulance man sat on, and drawers and machines and tubes and wires, and –

'Mrs Banbury!'

'I hope you don't mind, Elodie, but I would very much like to come with you.' That was nice of her, because I'd begun to feel as if I knew her a little, so she was a comfort. And she talked as we drove all the way to the hospital, which helped me because it was a lot of effort to think and talk at the same time as putting up with the pain, even though the pain wasn't as bad now.

'I've always wanted to ride in an ambulance!' said Mrs Banbury. 'I do love my house and my garden, of course, but it would be such *fun* to get out and about a bit more. I'm not allowed to drive myself around in a car these days. Poor eyesight, you see, so they are quite right not to let me.' Mrs Banbury's voice dropped, as if she was talking more to herself than to anybody else. 'Whether I can even keep living in my house is now in some doubt, according to my children. It's too much for me, really ... ' Her eyes were staring sadly at nothing very much.

'Couldn't you get help?' I said. 'I mean, I know it costs lots of money to pay somebody to do gardening and cleaning and things, but, er, have you got money?' Mum would have been glaring at me for asking something that was very definitely none of my business and probably rude and cheeky too. But it was what I was thinking, so I was just being honest, wasn't I? Mrs Banbury didn't seem to mind the question.

'Oh, yes, I have got money!' she said. 'I've actually got rather a lot, and not a penny of it earned by me. It's all thanks to my husband.' She frowned. 'Unfortunately that was how things were when I was younger. Funny how that dear man gave me so much over the years, and yet – ' I could tell she still wanted to get out and do things, even though she was really, really old.

'My dad could help you when he's not at work,' I told her. 'He's a chauffeur sometimes. But his car is very old-fashioned.'

'Could he? Is it?' Mrs Banbury sat up straighter. 'Is that truly a possibility?' So I told her about Dad and Betsy, the car that had been his dad's and *his* dad's before that. Then, suddenly, we were at the hospital and the doors were opening.

I was wheeled inside. And there was Mum in her blue scrubs and with a lanyard around her neck.

'Oh, Elodie!' she said. And we both burst into tears.

Chapter Eight

They cut off my trousers, X-rayed my leg and said I would need to have an operation to line up the broken bones. So I had to stay a night in the hospital. Dad came, bringing the list of my things Mum had told him to bring. Then he took Mrs Banbury home. She'd stayed with me and Mum all the way through the X-rays and things. She told Mum not to worry, and Mum explained to her what the doctors were doing, and some of the time I think they just forgot about me because they were chatting so much. That was nice, actually. I liked to think of Mrs Banbury having a ride home in Betsy.

Mum left me in my bed on the ward quite late at night, promising to be back in the morning before my operation. I was just snoozing into sleep, thinking about things backwards; what it was like, lying in the bushes with the cat licking me, then falling, then walking along that wall, and ...

'The swimming team!' I said out loud, and everyone in the other beds looked over at me. 'I can't swim!' I said, and they all looked at me as if they thought I was very strange. So I closed my eyes so that I couldn't see their faces, knowing that my one chance of winning pride for my family had gone *phut,* just like everything else I ever did. I had to breathe hard not to cry.

They did my leg operation the next day. By late afternoon I was ready to go home, my left leg in a bright clean plaster cast wrapped in blue bandages. They let me choose the colour.

I was interested to see what happens at hospitals, and of course Mum, dressed as Mum now, was talking to everybody because she knew some of them from her work. She explained things to me and fetched me a sandwich, and soon I was wheeled out of the hospital, clutching the crutches I had to learn to walk with.

'Here's Dad,' said Mum, and there was Betsy purring up to the hospital entrance.

I felt really tired, which Mum said was normal. And it was really hard hopping up those three staircases to our flat, even with Mum and Dad helping me. So then I went to bed and just slept and slept, not waking until the sun was on my face the next morning.

It was half-term, so I would have been off school anyway for those first days after the operation. I was mostly stuck in the flat, always sitting or lying down. Toby came over one afternoon.

'How are the kittens?' I asked.

'Very sweet,' he said. 'Mabel picked each of them up by taking the saggy bit of fur at the back of their necks into her mouth, and she took them to a new nest she's made for them in the wash basket, right on top of all the dirty washing. They're moving around a bit more, but not up on their legs yet. They sort of swim around on their tummies. They've opened their eyes, and their eyes are all bright blue. Look!' And he showed me some photos he'd taken on his phone. They weren't very good pictures, but I could see the blue eyes and which of the kittens was the little ginger one. I touched the photo and wished I could stroke the kitten for real.

Toby looked at me. 'Don't look so fed up, El!' he said. Then he remembered something. 'Oh, yes! Your mum and dad asked me to find out whether or not you like surprises. I don't think they wanted me to ask you straight out, but I don't know how else to do it.' See? Honest and straightforward; that's Toby.

'Well, I don't like falling-off-a-wall sorts of surprises!' I said. 'But I do like nice ones. What are they thinking of?'

'No idea,' said Toby. 'Probably something to do with your birthday. That's next week, isn't it? Do you know what you're getting?'

No, I didn't. But Grandma was coming soon after and she was going to need my room. I looked around. Clothes and toys and books were stuffed into every bit of it, and some of them were ones I'd grown out of. *At least I can make my bedroom nicer for Grandma so that it doesn't embarrass Mum so much,* I thought. So, when Toby had gone, I did some throwing out and moving things, trying to make space for Grandma's suitcase and bits.

'Are you packing?' said Dad, coming in all bouncy.

'Just tidying for when Grandma is in here,' I said.

'Oh, of course,' said Dad, as if he'd forgotten all about her coming to stay. He was in an odd mood. So was Mum. Sort of excited. Maybe it was because Grandma was on her way. Or maybe they really did have a nice secret ready for my birthday. You know that thing when you go into a room and suddenly the conversation that has been going on stops, and then somebody says something about the weather or asks who wants a cup of tea? That was happening a lot. I soon learned to move about silently on my crutches, not putting the plastered foot down, *clump*, but just swinging it as I hopped. The crutches had rubber ends, so they were quiet. I sneaked into the kitchen.

'But Elodie will have to – ' Mum was saying, then she shut her mouth, making an odd face at Dad before starting again: 'Er, Elodie will have to make sure she does her physio exercises if she wants that leg to mend quickly.'

Later, when Mum walked out on to the stairs when I came into the sitting room and she was on the phone, I *knew* she was talking about something secret.

'Who were you talking to?' I asked, when she came back inside.

'Never you mind,' she said.

But I *do* mind when people keep secrets from me, even if they might be nice ones. I wished I'd told Toby to say that I hate *all* secrets. But Mum and Dad were clearly enjoying their side of it, so I didn't tell them they had to tell me what was going on. My birthday was only days away, and I could wait.

What I was really, really hoping was that I was going to get you-know-what. But was that possible? A kitten has to be six weeks old before it can leave its mother. Perhaps they'd give me an IOU for a kitten, though? The waiting to find out was agony!

At last it actually *was* my birthday morning. I woke too early and began smiling straight away, lying in bed and watching the minutes tick towards seven o'clock when Mum and Dad's alarm clock would go off, and then, presumably, I'd discover what the secret thing was at last.

Mum always insists on breakfast before presents because that's what Grandma made them do when Mum was a girl. Honestly, how can you eat breakfast, even pain au chocolat, when you know there might be a kitten, or the promise of a kitten, waiting for you?

'We couldn't wrap up your present,' said Dad.

'Well, you can't wrap up something that's alive!' I said. Mum and Dad exchanged looks.

'You're right,' said Dad, looking surprised.

'Now, Elodie,' said Mum, beginning at last to clear the plates and mugs into the dishwasher. 'Your present is going to need looking after, feeding and—'

'Oh, where is he – I mean it?'

'Look in our bedroom,' smiled Dad.

And I was off my chair and hobbling without crutches, but holding on to the back of a chair and wall and a door handle, hurrying over to Mum and Dad's room that was cluttered with boxes full of stuff, clearing the flat ready for Grandma's visit. But what my brain was whirling around with was wondering whether or not they knew which of the kittens at Toby's was 'my' special one? Or, since the kittens were so young, perhaps they'd got me another cat? Perhaps a second-hand rescue sort of a cat? My heart tore just a little bit at the thought that my present might be an old cat instead of that teeny ginger kitten. But I darned that rip in my heart back together again by thinking how, until last week, I would have been delighted with *any* cat. I could, I *would*, love whatever cat it was. I took a deep breath.

There, on Mum and Dad's bed, was what looked like a box draped with one of Mum's bright scarves instead of wrapping paper. Pinned to the scarf was a card that said:

For our darling Elodie
Happy birthday!

'Hello?' I said, quietly so as not to frighten whoever was in that box. Had my clomping into the room been scary? 'Sorry to frighten you.' There was silence. Poor scared thing! 'You can come out of the box now,' I whispered. 'Are you ready for the daylight?' Carefully, gently, I lifted up Mum's scarf, and there was ...

... a wooden box full of soil, with one rather boring-looking green-leafed plant in the middle of it.

I felt as if all my insides had slipped down my body to below my knees.

'Had you guessed?' said Mum. 'Dad thought you probably had!'

'Um, is it a litter tray?' I asked. But the plant showed for just about certain that it wasn't. Mum laughed.

'It's a window box, Elodie! Your very own mini garden! Look, there are seeds as well as the zinnia!' She pointed to the little flat packets beside the box of soil. There was a shiny new trowel too. 'Sow those seeds, water and nurture them, and they'll grow into a bright show of flowers. Herbs too, for cooking, if you like. You can enjoy the magic of nature as those little dots of seeds grow and change, until they explode like slow fireworks into coloured flowers and

wonderful smells and delicious tastes and, well, beauty!'
I told you she gets rapturous when she talks about
gardening. She clearly thought it was the best present ever.
'They'll look so bright and pretty at the window, here or,
well, anywhere!'

So, my parents not only didn't know me well enough
to know what I'd truly like as a present, but they were
planning for me to leave home!

I sat down on the bed.

'Leg hurting?' said Dad. I looked at him. His and
Mum's faces looked like mine felt when I gave Mum that
pasta necklace back when I was four, and I was so *sure* that
it was the perfect present for Mum. So I smiled at them.

'Thank you,' I said. 'Really, thank you!'

'I knew you'd love it!' said Mum. 'You were so keen to
help me with planting the other day. Right,' she glanced at
her watch. 'I've got lots to do today.'

'What?' I said, hoping she'd at least ask what sort of
cake I wanted for tea. Toby was coming over for it.

'Oh, just getting everything sorted, you know, for
Grandma coming next week,' she said, folding up her
scarf and adding it to a pile of other ones on her chest of
drawers. She'd got some study leave away from lectures
and the hospital for a few days. I thought it was a shame
those days didn't coincide with when her mum was

going to be here, but she was still fussing about getting everything just right to impress Grandma.

'Is Grandma going to be in this room instead of mine, then? Because of my leg?' That added guilt to the different flavours of emotion swilling around in me.

'She might,' said Mum. 'Now, come on, chip chop, Elodie. Are you up to school today?'

I promise you, it was easier leaving the flat and going to school than it would have been if there *had* been a kitten in that box. I struggled down the three flights of steps, *thump-bump,* forty-five times over. And the thumping and bumping gave me a thinking rhythm. What I thought was that, even though my own parents clearly didn't know me as well as they thought they did, *I* still wanted to make my grandma's visit as good as possible, especially for Mum. Perhaps I could still give *them* a lovely surprise present of something to be proud of me for?

'Dad, please can you fetch me the red bag that's under my bed? I need it for today,' I said.

'Anything you want, m'lady,' said Dad. 'Is there anything else I can get you? A tiara, perhaps? Or some caviar on toast? Or—'

'Yes! Thanks for reminding me! Can you shove a bin bag into it? And that wide silver tape you use on the car?'

'But, what—?'

'A school thing. Pretty please?'

'All right,' said Dad. 'Today, my dear, you can have anything.'

Except a kitten, I thought, as I *thump-bumped* on down the stairs.

Chapter Nine

When I arrived at school in Betsy, with my crutches and my leg in plaster, I was suddenly the person that everyone was looking at, and then talking to, wanting to know what had happened to my leg. Toby stepped forward to be beside me, and he told everybody all about my fall, but made it sound much more dramatic than it was. 'This huge cat came at her like a charging rhino, knocking her off the wall that was way up high, so she crashed down, falling on to her leg so that – SNAP! – ' Toby made a face and mimed snapping something in half with his hands, 'her leg was broken.'

'Urgh!' went everyone. 'Did it hurt?'

'Then – Weeeooooo! – ' Toby's hands snapped open and shut to demonstrate the flashing lights of the ambulance, 'the ambulance came, and—'

'That's enough,' said Mr Sim, who was on playground duty. 'Off to your classes, please, everyone.'

So, momentarily, I was the centre of attention, but not in a way that would make your mum or grandma proud; not when it was for falling off a wall that you shouldn't have got up on to in the first place. I gripped my red bag tight and *thump-hopped* into school.

'Oh, Elodie!' said Miss Evans when she saw me.

'Good morning, Miss Evans,' I said. I gave her a wide-eyed smile of the sort that Grace does to make grown-ups melt. 'It's nothing big, really. I know I need crutches for walking, but I'll still be fine for the swimming trials.' And I bent my leg to show that it could still kick, even if it hurt a bit. I tried to keep smiling instead of wincing.

'Don't be preposterous, Elodie,' said Miss Evans.

'Why not?'

'Because, obviously,' said Miss Evans, 'your plaster cast will get soggy and disintegrate. I'm quite sure the hospital would not approve.'

'But I've got a bin liner and my dad's waterproof duct tape to seal the bag on to my leg to keep the plaster dry. Honestly, it will work!'

'No, Elodie,' she said. 'Absolutely not.' Then she turned to the class and clapped her hands. 'Settle down, everyone. We will do our Monday Spelling Quiz.' And that was that. Miss Evans calls it a 'quiz' to hide that it's a test, but nobody is fooled by that.

So we did the test. I didn't do very well. Of course. I hadn't even looked at the spellings, what with the hospital stuff and my birthday, and anyway I had been thinking test results didn't matter if I could just get a swimming trophy … which Miss Evans clearly didn't want me to have. 'It's preposterous,' I muttered, because I rather liked that word.

'Did you have something to say, Elodie?' asked Miss Evans.

'No, Miss.'

When Miss Evans rounded up the people to try out for the swimming team at lunchtime, I tagged along. She raised an eyebrow at me, pushed her mouth together, but said nothing.

'Why come, when she's said you're not allowed to swim?' said Toby. 'Why are you taking your bag?'

'Because,' I said, 'maybe somebody will get ill, or slip and break a leg ... Er, well something like that. And then they'll *need* me for the team, and she won't even worry about the bin liner thing.'

Miss Evans heard me say that. 'You are incorrigible, Elodie,' she said.

Why shouldn't I be incorrigible? Miss Evans is always telling me that I'll 'get there in the end' if I 'persevere'. Well, what's the difference between persevering and being incorrigible, I want to know?

I sat on a hard plastic seat at the end of a row, sort of sideways so that my plastered leg could rest more comfortably. I crossed my arms, breathed the chloriney air and listened to the shouts and splashes as I watched the others taking turns to swim races, doing different strokes. Either Grace or Toby were fastest for breaststroke, crawl and backstroke. Robin came last in them all. I felt sorry for Robin because I know how that feels, but, oh, I was almost shouting out with frustration because I *knew* that, even with a leg plaster slowing me down, I'd have been faster than him. But ...

'We need eight in the team, so that means each of you swimmers has made the grade!' said Miss Evans, as if that was a great triumph and not just taking the only choice she had. Then she looked over to me. 'And we will have one more member of our team.'

Oh, wow, Miss Evans, I love you! I thought. All that time she'd just been pretending to be mean and fierce after all, and now suddenly I was panicking a bit because, actually, *was* I going to be able to swim with one heavy leg in flappy plastic? But, hang on, what was she saying?

'Yes, I'm appointing Elodie as our swimming team's official reporter.'

Reporter?

'What?' I said, because I really didn't know what she was talking about.

'To watch the races and then to write a report for the school's website,' said Miss Evans. 'You will be integral to the team, Elodie.'

Never mind being integral, she *knew* I wasn't good at spelling! I'd do it wrong, and everyone would read it and laugh, and, oh, couldn't she *see* that was her worst idea ever? I tried to lumber to my feet.

'Brilliant!' said Toby. 'That means you can come with us to the gala!' Then he saw my face, and his face went from a slice-of-melon smile to a little grape-sized 'o'. 'What's the matter?'

Well, I wasn't going to announce to all of them – staring at me now and waiting for an answer – that I couldn't spell or write well enough, was I? 'Nothing's the matter,' I muttered. That was a lie, but Toby's smile widened out again.

So I was stuck with being the swimming team reporter.

On top of that, Mum had bought those not-as-nice-as-they-look chocolate muffins from the shop for my birthday tea, because she was too busy sorting the flat to cook a proper birthday cake.

Chapter Ten

When I arrived at the gala on Saturday, everywhere was noisy with children and teachers and parents, all echoey under the pool roof. They'd put up bunting over the pool to make it look special.

I sat with Toby's mum and dad and sister in the hard blue seats. We could look down on our team and Miss Evans. I'd come with Toby's family because Mum and Dad were too busy, and actually I was glad of that. There was no point in them coming when they wouldn't see me winning anything.

I'd got my notebook with me and a pen. 'Swimming Gala', I wrote on the top of the page. *What did Miss Evans want me to write?* I wondered. Just notes of who won what, or more than that?

'Miss Evans!' I shouted, but she was too far away to hear.

'What do you need?' said Toby's mum.

'To know what to write,' I said.

'I'd write down everything, if I were you, and then you can cut out anything you don't need later,' she said. That was easy for her to say. She didn't know how hard it was to write if you were me! I did try to do what she said, but I got stuck straight away.

The people for the first race, including Robin for our school, had to dive in to start.

'On your marks, get set, go!' said the man, and *splash* – in they went. Except that the sound they made wasn't really *splash*. It went on for longer than that. It was more of a *sploosh* followed by a gentle *splash splash*, as their feet kicked in the water. And by the time I'd decided on those words, the race had finished and I didn't even know who'd won ... except that Robin was still breaststroking to the end after the others had begun to get out. So I was clearly as rubbish at reporting as he was at swimming. No surprise there.

I tried to write more, and faster, with each race. Our school wasn't winning anything. And then it came to the last race and that had Toby doing crawl, which he's good at.

'To-bi!' I shouted. 'To-bi! To-bi!' Cherry, and then Toby's mum and dad, joined in with the chanting. 'To-bi!' But then I remembered my job, and I tried to write down everything that happened just as it was. And Toby won! I enjoyed that.

The other good thing was that I got to go to Toby's house again, so I got to see the kittens. Better than that, I was allowed to hold them. They were silky shiny soft, and their eyes opened and looked around, all big and blue.

'Hello, Puisìn,' I said to the little ginger one, saying the word the way Dad had: 'Pwisheen'.

'What did you call him?' said Toby.

'Puisìn means "puss" in Irish. Dad told me,' I said.

'Would you like to have that kitten?' said Toby. 'We're going to give that one and the ginger and black-and-white one away and just keep the white one.'

'I'd *love* to have him,' I said. 'But Mum and Dad won't let me.' The kitten opened its pink mouth and gave the tiniest, squeakiest 'meow'. His ears were tiny triangles that looked as though they'd slipped down the side of his head. His tail was another triangle, but longer and slim. And the teeny little pink paw pads on each foot were – oh, I don't know what they were, but they made me ache with wanting to have him as mine.

I got to stay over at Toby's that night because Mum and Dad were busy with work or something, so I had lots of time with the kittens that evening and the next morning.

Toby's dad always does pancakes for breakfast on Sundays. Pancakes as well as kittens! Then Toby's mum gave a shout, 'Elodie, your parents are here!'

'Please, would it be all right to show them the kittens?' I said. Surely if Mum saw and stroked them she *couldn't* resist saying 'yes' to Puisìn, could she?

'Of course,' said Toby's mum. But that's not what

happened. I *thump-bumped* to meet Mum and Dad at the door, and ...

'Dad! What are you doing?' He came towards me with a whole roll of purple and pink flowery wrapping paper, and he began to wrap it around me. 'Mum?' But she was taking my crutches from my hands. 'What?'

'Hold still!' said Dad.

'Mum, what's Dad doing?' But Mum had got a giant roll of sticky tape, and she was following Dad, circling around me, wrapping me in paper and tape from my legs up. Before I could escape, they'd pinned my arms to my sides. 'Hey!'

Toby's family had all come to see what was happening, and I saw Toby's laughing face before it suddenly disappeared from view, and all I could see was paper.

'I'll suffocate!'

'No, you won't,' said Mum. 'We'll leave the top and bottom open.'

'But WHAT ARE YOU DOING?' I didn't shout because I didn't want to frighten the kittens in the box not far away, but I did try to sound firm. It was a bit scary, not being able to see anything and having my arms stuck to my sides so that I couldn't put them out to break a fall, especially with one leg in plaster so I was already wobbly. But somebody – Dad, I think – had a firm hold of my

shoulders as the last of the tape screeched around me, then was snipped to finish it off.

Apart from my feet, I was in a sort of tube of paper, and, because of that tape, I couldn't escape from it.

'OK, Elodie?' said Dad.

'No!' I said. They were all laughing, but it didn't feel funny to me.

'We've got another birthday present for you,' said Mum. 'It's a bit late and it's far too big to wrap up, so we've wrapped you up instead.'

'What do you mean?' What could be far bigger than me? *Not a kitten,* I thought, and hope deflated inside me like an old balloon. I tried to poke a finger through the paper.

'Oi, don't tear the paper and spoil the surprise!' said Dad. 'Keep still!'

Honestly, what were my parents thinking? Have you ever heard of parents wrapping their ten-, I mean eleven-year-old daughter up in paper? And then making a sort of seat from their four hands, clutching each other and telling the 'daughter parcel' to sit? Can you imagine what that feels like for the parcel person? It was scary and weird and exciting and, well, the strangest thing I've ever felt because I just didn't properly believe it was happening. My face had paper up against it, and paper was all around me so that it scrumpled and scrunched when I moved at all, and it tore – *riiip!* – right across my backside when I sat down on their hands.

'Just trust us!' said Mum, and that made me laugh, and that made the paper crinkle more.

'I don't!' I said. 'Please can I have my arms out? Please? *They* can't see anything!'

So when they set me down again, they each tore a hole in one side to let my arms out. I grabbed around for something solid to hold on to. I think I punched Dad in the stomach. 'Oof' he went, but he was laughing along with everyone else.

I don't know why I didn't just tear the paper off myself. That's what my hands wanted to do, but they stayed clinging to Mum on one side and Dad on the other because, well, because I hadn't heard my mum and dad having such a giggle together for a very long time, and I was loving it at the same time as being frightened and embarrassed and, oh, everything you can imagine if it was you in that situation.

'Now sit again,' said Mum, twisting me as I went down, and I knew it was on to one of Betsy's big leather seats. Soon I was strapped in, the door clunked shut, and I started to float forwards as the engine purred. Without being able to see anything, I was suddenly really aware of all the sounds. The engine changed its sound when Dad changed gear, Mum was whispering and giggling, and there were sudden siren noises or the roar of a motorbike from outside. Then I felt the car loll me sideways as it turned to the left, and the sound changed to something crunchy and the traffic noises stopped.

'Where are we?' I said.

'Just wait. Not long now!' Mum's voice was a bit breathless because she was excited. But about what? Betsy was slowing down, then stopped, and a moment later the door clunked open, and I was being unstrapped and pulled off the seat. There was another voice I could hear now.

'Mrs Banbury?' I said, even more confused. Was this some kind of surprise party, perhaps?

'Yes, it's me!' Mrs Banbury was as excited and giggly as Mum and Dad were.

'I'm wrapped up,' I told her, a bit pointlessly, because she could obviously see that for herself.

'I know!' she said. 'Such a jape!' That wasn't a word I knew, but I could tell it meant something funny in a mischievous way.

Hands moved me around a bit, then Dad said, 'All right, then. This is the countdown to opening your present, El. Ten, nine ... ' Mum and Mrs Banbury had joined in. But I was fed up with being the victim in all this, so I just grabbed and tore at the paper around me and didn't wait for the 'three, two, one'. I pulled the paper from in front of my face and saw ...

'What? Where are we?'

The three of us were standing beside Betsy, and there was a house in front of us.

'Home!' said Mum, and she burst into tears. 'This is our new home!'

Chapter Eleven

'But – !' I looked at Dad, who was just grinning and nodding, and there were tears on his cheeks too. Mrs Banbury took my arm in her twiggy soft old hands.

'Come and see,' she said.

I stepped out of the paper tube and Mum handed me my crutches from the car. I went with Mrs Banbury, listening to her talk as if she was somehow far away, because my brain was fizzing with trying to make sense of everything.

'This cottage has been empty for a while. When my husband and I first moved into the house, my sister lived here for a bit, and after she moved away we rented it out to various people over the years. My last tenant left last year, and I've never got around to advertising for a new one because I was advised by an estate agent that nobody would be interested in the place until it was completely repainted and so on. But now your family is to rent it, Elodie. I'm delighted – I really wanted people that I know to be the new tenants. The garden is even more run-down than the house is, I'm afraid. But your mother tells me that she might enjoy taming that.'

'She loves gardening!' I said. 'But where are we?' I suddenly wondered if we were miles from the people and places I loved. It was so hard to tell how far the car had travelled when I'd been wrapped as a parcel.

'You have actually been in this garden before,' said Mrs Banbury. She pointed at my leg. 'Not that long ago.' And I realized.

'On the other side of Reginald's wall?'

'Do you mean the cat? Priss? Exactly. I live over there in a house that is far too big for one old lady, but it's my home. Mine and Priscilla's.' And then she invited me into the house that was going to be my home.

The house smelled old, but in a nice way. The stained glass in the door meant that when the sun shone, the colours jumped out of the glass and on to the walls and floor of the hallway. 'Go upstairs and find your room,' said Mum.

So, *thump-clump*, I went up the dark wood stairs. They changed direction halfway up. There was a stained-glass window at that halfway point too, letting in more light and colours. And at the top of the stairs there were four closed doors. 'Like an advent calendar!' I said.

'Open them!' said Mrs Banbury. 'I believe your new room is a late birthday present for you.'

It did feel like opening presents, opening those doors to discover what was behind them. The first door opened on to a big old-fashioned bathroom with a bath that had metal lion's feet. The second door opened into a bedroom with a big window that overlooked the garden and then on, over the wall to the buildings I knew on the street. You could even see a glimpse of our block of flats ... with the third-floor flat that presumably wasn't 'ours' any more. The bed in this room was Mum and Dad's one.

'So that's why you've been doing so much packing up!' I said.

'We've been working non-stop with a hired van while you were at the gala and Toby's,' said Dad, following me in.

The third door I opened was to a smaller room that was mostly full of boxes.

'Is this—?'

'No,' said Mum. 'This is the room we need to sort very quickly for Grandma to stay in.'

'So, then – ?' I *thump-bumped* across to open the last of the four doors, and ...

'Oh!' I said, and it was an 'oh' in a really, really good way. 'It's just ... Oh!' And I smiled so wide it hurt my cheeks! Because this room with my bed in it had a sloping ceiling on one side with a window in it, and on the other side there were tall glass French-window doors, open on to a view of the garden and Mrs Banbury's house, AND ...

'A balcony! Mine? Can I step on to it?'

'Isn't it nice?' said Mrs Banbury. 'My sister had these doors put in when they added a newer kitchen downstairs. So your balcony is the kitchen's roof.'

'Your box of flowers can go on here,' said Mum. 'Your own mini garden.'

'It's all perfect!' I said, and hugged her hard. Suddenly that box full of soil and promise *was* the perfect present after all. I turned to Mrs Banbury and hugged her too.

She laughed. 'I'm just so grateful to you, Elodie, for introducing yourself and your parents to me. I'm so pleased the house will be lived in again.'

For tea, Mum, Dad and I had peanut-butter sandwiches and crisps and apples, sitting on the floor of the kitchen with our backs leaning against the wall because the table and chairs were all covered in boxes of stuff.

We walked – well I *thump-clumped* – into the garden before bedtime. I thought the garden was huge, with lots of green and flowery things. Mum started pointing to particular ones.

'Poppies,' she said. 'And roses. Look at the foxgloves just beginning to flower!' Then she said, 'Grandma flies in tomorrow,' and she didn't seem stressed about it, even though Grandma's room wasn't nearly ready for her yet. I could see that she was proud of this home, even though the garden wasn't a tidy one – yet. I still wished that I could make her feel proud of me too, though.

Chapter Twelve

'Well, bless me, is that little Elodie?' said Grandma's loud voice, booming out so that everybody in the airport seemed to turn and look to see 'little' me. 'My, how tall you are! And what in the world have you done to that leg, girl? Tell me, but first of all give me a hug – come on, quick, quick, quick!'

Grandma thought I had grown so tall, but to me, she had shrunk. The top of her head came up to my nose! Of course, we'd seen each other on computer screens, but she was always sitting down with those shelves of trophies behind her. It was so nice to hug her, to be wrapped up in her warmth and to hear her laugh bubbling into my shoulder. Then she was hugging Mum, then hugging Dad, then hugging me again.

'Still this old car?' she said as Dad opened Betsy's door. 'GOOD!'

'But not the same old flat we've been living in recently,' said Dad.

'Also GOOD,' said Grandma, settling into the front passenger seat as Mum slipped in beside me in the back. Grandma always has strong opinions. And she hadn't even *seen* our new house yet!

Our new, but old, home was filled with talk, talk, talk

and lots of laughing from then on. Mrs Banbury came over with a coffee and walnut cake she'd made to welcome Grandma, and the two of them yakked away as Mum and Dad scurried about, still unpacking and putting things in places. We hadn't enough furniture from the flat to fill the house properly, but there were two armchairs, which was lucky.

'Tell me all about Trinidad,' said Mrs Banbury. 'I want to close my eyes and imagine that I'm there!'

That set Grandma off, telling all about the wonders of the clear sea, the freshly caught fish, the fruits on the trees, the flowers and the calypso music. Then she suddenly clapped her hands, making poor Mrs Banbury jump and open her eyes. 'You know what?' said Grandma. 'Britain is wonderful too, especially when it has my beautiful, clever daughter. She's working to be a doctor, you know. Passing all the exams, top of the class. And such a good mother as well!' And on she went, boasting. Then she turned to me. 'Elodie, do you make your mother as proud of you as I am of her? I'm sure you do! What is it that you are good at, Elodie?'

I felt myself go hot. What could I say?

'So shy!' laughed Grandma. 'I will find out soon enough, no doubt.' She swept both arms out wide to show she thought I'd show her something big and exciting, and

... *crash!* She knocked Mrs Banbury's mug of tea off the table, splurting brown wetness all over Mrs Banbury.

'Oh, I am so clumsy!' said Grandma. I was glad that got her off the subject of *me*! I hobbled to find a cloth. But when I came back with it, Mum had got the subject round to me again.

'You can come to Elodie's school assembly tomorrow, Mumma,' she told Grandma. 'Elodie is going to read out her report on the swimming gala.'

'No, really, don't bother!' I said. 'It'll be boring. Soooo boring. Anyway, you don't want to sit on those diddy little chairs, Grandma. Get Dad to take you somewhere in Betsy. With Mrs Banbury? That would be much nicer.'

'I will come to your school,' said Grandma, in a way that showed the decision was final.

'Do you think it would possibly be acceptable for me to also attend?' said Mrs Banbury. 'It would be such a treat!'

Oh no! is what I thought of that.

* * *

So, next morning, there I was on the stage, dressed in my green and grey, my usual orange Afro hair in braids for the first time in years because Grandma said that was a proper hair arrangement for a girl about to speak on stage. I didn't mind the braids. It was reading out my Swimming Gala report that was scaring me. I'd left my crutches on the floor beside my chair. My hands, holding the paper, were shaking a bit. I'd woken early in my lovely bedroom, gone and sat on a rocking chair on my balcony and practised reading it out loud. So I wasn't so worried about reading it because I knew it almost by heart. I was just embarrassed already because I knew that it wouldn't be any good.

Suddenly the headmistress was saying: 'And now over to you, Elodie.' It felt like something from television news: 'Over to our correspondent Elodie Taylor in the Aquatic Centre.' The hall had gone silent. The only way to get it all over with was for me to begin talking. So I read about the gala in general and the early races, which I did quite quickly. Then it came to that last race with Toby in it, and I actually forgot that anybody was listening to me because the writing took me back to exactly how it had felt when I was there, watching …

'"Go!" said the starter, and the five racers from the five schools reached forward, their ten arms in five upside-down "V" shapes, so they were like the fronts of ships, slicing the water to open and let them in. *Sploosh!* They reached and scooped and kicked and twisted to grab breaths with sideways mouths, all five of them kicking the water into splashy waves behind them. At first, the boy in a red swimming hat was in front, with three in a row just behind him, then one more getting left further behind with every second. But our Toby was getting a tiny bit closer every moment to that red-hat boy. He was scooping and kicking and hardly even bothering to grab breaths! Could he catch the leader up? Could he overtake him? I clutched the back of the seat in front of me. "To-bi!" I shouted, and it felt as if my shout shot invisibly through the air to push him just enough forward because – yes! – then he *was* just ahead, and – yes! – he touched the end of the pool first. He won! "YAAAAY!" shouted everyone at our school's end of the seats, with the swimming-pool echo making that double the usual yaaaay sound. Everyone else looked glum as gooseberries or made their mouths do little polite smiles and their hands do little polite claps, but they knew their schools had lost that race to the best swimmer from the best school: Toby and Elm Street Primary! So hooray for all our team. And, most of all, hooray for Toby Wythenshaw, who did the swimming for us all. We are proud of you, Toby.'

That was the end of it, so I stopped and looked up from my piece of paper. Everyone was looking at me in silence. They had wide eyes and mouths a bit open like baby birds in a nest waiting for worms. Then ...

'Oh, Elodie!' said my grandma, loud and proud, and she started clapping, and that clapping spread like the spilled tea, over and across the hall until everyone was clapping and cheering for what Toby had done.

'Stand up, Toby!' I shouted, and he did stand up, and they all turned to look at him and cheer. That was a relief, and it was lovely. I clapped and cheered him too.

Then Miss Evans came on to the stage, and she held her hands up for quiet. I turned to go and sit down with everyone else, but Miss Evans put a hand on my shoulder, and then she spoke to everyone sitting in front of us.

'Strictly speaking, Elodie's report was full of errors. You should never start a sentence with "and", for instance. And I'm not sure you're allowed to make up your own words.'

'Why not?' I said, without thinking about where I was. '*Somebody* must have made up every word once, so why can't I? And you just started *your* sentence with "and" as well!' Why was I arguing with a teacher, on stage, in front of my grandma and Mrs Banbury? Oh, no!

'Well.' Miss Evans looked a bit startled. 'Um, yes I did, but that was speech rather than writing, and the rules for each are different.'

'Wh – ' I began, then I slapped a hand over my mouth to shut myself up. Everybody was laughing. As usual.

Oh, I wanted to get off that stage and hide! But Miss Evans went on.

'What I *was* going to say, and *will* now say, is that I think your Swimming Gala report is brilliant, Elodie. Truly brilliant.'

'Oh, Elodie, I knew it!' That was Grandma, and then everyone was laughing and clapping all over again before I finally got to limp off the stage.

Phew!

I sort of hummed inside with happiness all the rest of that day, remembering the smiles and clapping.

Chapter Thirteen

Grandma stayed with us for four weeks, helping sort out our new home, telling Mum what to do with the overgrown garden and going on trips with Mrs Banbury. I had to keep going to school, of course, but it was mostly quite fun, heading for the end of primary school, with no more important tests to do. Of course, my test results weren't anywhere near as good as Toby's results. But Grandma didn't *seem* to be too disappointed in me in spite of that. So I asked her, 'Do you mind very much that I still haven't got a trophy or certificate to give you for your shelf collection?' She smiled wide and laughed.

'Elodie, don't you realize that the cups-and-medals kind of winning isn't the only, or even the best, kind of triumph life can give us? I've got grandsons and granddaughters back home who get those things for maths competitions or running races or for ballet or spelling bees, or for I don't know what. I put those cups and medals on display, and I dust them. Do they make me proud? Sure. But you know what, Elodie?'

'What?'

'The best running race I watched in my whole life for making me so full of pride it pretty near burst my dress open was the race I watched you in when you were just four years old.'

'That was years and years ago! *And* I came last out of everybody in it!'

'Sure you did. But Elodie, you did something then that was better than winning some race that doesn't mean anything to anyone beyond a bit of fun at nursery school. Remember *why* you came last?'

And suddenly I did ... but Grandma wanted to tell me the tale as if I hadn't been there or known anything about it. She was telling me as if she was telling friends back home. I realized that must be because she *did* tell her friends that same story, probably over and over again. Perhaps she *was* proud? But why?

'Little Elodie, in her blue shorts and white T-shirt, was running as fast as she could. And she could run faster than most of those little ones. My Elodie was running right at the front, when all of a sudden, a boy behind her tripped and fell. She heard him cry out, and she stopped, and all those other children just ran on past the two of them. They must have heard and seen the boy too, but they were so intent on winning that race, they just kept on running. But not my Elodie! Oh, no. My Elodie stopped. She bent down and she pulled that boy up on to his feet again.'

'It was Toby,' I remembered.

Grandma wanted to complete the tale. 'My little Elodie

held that little boy Toby's hand, and then the two of them ran together, awkward as anything because they were so close they were almost tripping each other up, but they were smiling and happy! And they crossed that finish line after all the other children finished, but they were laughing together.' Grandma grinned wide and clapped her hands. 'Remember who got the loudest cheer that day, Elodie?'

'I bet Grace Meadows won the race, didn't she? She still wins any running race.'

Grandma laughed. 'A big girl won the race, sure. Maybe your Grace, I don't remember much about her. She got cheers, but not the everybody-cheering-at-the-top-of-their-voices cheer that my Elodie got for helping another instead of going all out to win the race herself.'

Grandma sighed and shook her head as she smiled. 'I never was more proud in my life than at that moment. I tell you, girl, pride is a real joy when it's goodness you are proud of. Goodness, or skill of a kind that takes others with you into something joyful, as your poetry did today.'

'Poetry! That was a report, Grandma.'

'It was *poetry*,' insisted Grandma, slapping the table. 'Poetry is words with power to make you *feel*. You didn't win any swimming medals yourself, Elodie, but you told the story of that win in such a way that we shared that

winning as if every one of us had been at that pool with Toby! Even your old grandma felt she had swum that race herself and won! See, as well as being a brilliant poet, you're a natural sharer and carer, Elodie, just like your mumma, my Maureen, is. Perhaps that's the best thing anyone can be in life.'

That was nice.

The day before Grandma was due to fly home to Trinidad, she told me at breakfast that she wanted to give me a present.

'I brought one with me in my bag, but I'm so clumsy I broke it, so it went in the bin. Besides, now I see the girl you are, how grown-up and thoughtful you are, I'm not so sure that doll was right for you in any case. So let me get you something you really want. What in the world might that be?'

I froze for a moment. Did I dare tell the truth? I glanced at Mum. Dad was at work. I opened my mouth and said, 'A kitten?'

'A kitten?' said Grandma, and I couldn't tell whether that was in a good way or bad way.

'I really, *really* want a kitten,' I said. 'And I know just which one.'

'Uh-huh?' said Grandma. Then she sort of exploded into laughing!

'It's not a joke! I *do* want one!' I said, but she laughed and laughed, then finally caught enough breath to say, 'Well, *of course* you want a kitten, Elodie. It's in your blood! I've had cats all my life, and your mumma, my Maureen, was always bringing home some poor starving flea-bitten scrap of a cat that she wanted to nurse back to health. It's what set her on the road to medicine in the first place. Why didn't I think of a cat for you myself? That's perfect.'

'Mum?' I said.

Mum was smiling. She said to Grandma, 'Do you remember that black cat, the one I called Hoppy, who had just three legs? I loved him so much.'

'Mum?' I stood right in front of her so that she couldn't ignore me. 'I thought you didn't like cats!'

'Whatever made you think that?'

'Dad said you wouldn't let me have one!'

'Because the landlord of that flat said that cats were nasty dirty creatures who scratched paintwork and made a place smell. But that's not what *I* think.'

'So can we? Oh, pleeease, Mum? I know Dad would say yes.'

'Yes,' said Mum, as if nothing could be simpler.

Yes! One little word, just three letters long, but such a BIG word in what it can mean!

'Please can I borrow your phone, Mum? I need to ring Toby.'

Chapter Fourteen

The next day, Grandma flew home, but when I next spoke to her over the Internet I held Puisìn up to show her. Grandma clasped her hands together and said, 'Just beautiful. As you are, my Elodie.' And guess what? Behind her I could see the usual shelves of cups and medals and things, but right in the middle of them all was a framed photograph of me, standing on that school stage with my braids and white socks, reading out my Swimming Gala report. And I just *knew* she would be pointing to it and telling her friends a new story about how her granddaughter Elodie 'done good'.

* * *

I am thinking about it all as I weed my window box on my balcony now, making room in it to plant some catmint. Puisìn is asleep on the warm lead roof beside me, his orange fur shining and warm like golden syrup.

I suddenly remember Grandma saying, 'Oh, Elodie!' in that proud loud way, and I am smiling at the memory of it all over again.